Shape Your Identity

Crafting Success Habits with Purpose and Passion

Zachary V. King

Table of Contents

We are what we repeatedly do. Excellence, then, is not an act, but a habit.

— Aristotle

Chapter 1. Introduction

Introducing an invigorating Special Report titled "Shape Your Identity: Crafting Success Habits with Purpose and Passion!" This is your gateway to a transformed life, brimming with purpose and illuminated by passion. Delve into a world where habits aren't a chore, but a delightful compass, guiding you towards success. With this shouldn't-be-missed dossier, every day becomes a chance to grow, to develop, and to bring yourself in sync with your dreams and aspirations. Offering innovative insights into self-realization and habit formation, this captivating guide is not your typical self-help manuscript, but a profound, life-altering adventure! So why wait? Add this exciting Special Report to your cart right away, because your journey to a dynamic, passion-fuelled, purposeful life starts here, starts now!

Chapter 2. Understanding Identity: The Core of Success

The quest for success begins with an exploration of our own identity. This chapter embarks on a journey towards understanding the intricate dynamics of self-perception, self-awareness, and self-identity, and how these elements, interlaced, form the foundation of success and fulfillment. This journey will unveil the ways in which a more comprehensive grasp of one's identity can shape attitudes, beliefs, strategies, and ultimately, the tenacious pursuit of success.

2.1. Unraveling Selfhood: The First Step

The story of each individual's identity begins with the notion of 'self.' The 'self' is a complex amalgamation of our emotions, experiences, characteristics, ideals, values, and ambitions. It's a unique manifestation, a distinct entity, born from the substrate of our conscious and subconscious minds. The self, with its composite whims, ideas, and sentiments, intricately molds our identity.

Understanding our identity, therefore, requires an in-depth delineation of self. This process necessitates a commitment to self-reflection and introspection. By fostering a habit of routinely examining our thoughts, beliefs, emotions, actions, and reactions, we tread the path towards a more profound comprehension of our intimacies, peculiarities, and consistencies that constitute our identity.

2.2. Of Facets and Features: Dissecting Identity

Once we begin to uncover the layers of our self, the multifaceted nature of identity begins to emerge. It's not just about who we think we are, but also how we perceive ourselves in relation to others and the larger world. Recurring themes, recurring patterns of response towards certain stimuli, begin to surface, offering invaluable insights into our personal identity.

This section illustrates how our attitudes, beliefs, perceived social roles, inherent and acquired traits, all contribute towards designing the complex mosaic of our identity. Furthermore, it underlines how these aspects are intertwined, influencing and defining each other, thereby stressing the importance of examining these aspects holistically for a comprehensive understanding of our identity.

2.3. Reflections Mirror Reality: The Role of Self-Perception in Identity Formation

An integral part of forming our identity is how we perceive ourselves – our self-perception. It's the mirror which reflects our self-image, illustrating how we view our attributes and abilities. Self-perception, however, is not always a direct reflection of reality. It could be distorted or enhanced by our psychological and emotional state of mind, past experiences, and external influences.

This portion of the chapter underpins the critical role that self-perception plays in shaping our identity. It elucidates the dynamics between self-perception and identity, laying bare the repercussions of distorted self-perceptions. It also provides strategies to nurture a balanced, realistic self-perception, thus facilitating a resilient, authentic identity formation.

2.4. Identity Nurtures Success: The Core Connection

The culmination of this exploration is in the realization that our identity is closely linked to our success. For, our successes and bouts of triumph are generally the results of endeavors that resonate with our identity. They are often pursuits that are aligned with our values, beliefs, abilities, and skills – components that are rooted in our identity.

This part of the chapter unveils how understanding and embracing our identity can guide us in designing effective strategies for success. By engaging with our authentic selves and aligning our goals accordingly, we are more likely to persevere, resist distractions, overcome setbacks, and stay motivated–the tried and tested ingredients for lasting success.

So, as we delve deeper into understanding our identity, we pave the way for success ingrained with purpose and fueled by passion. It's a journey that calls for introspection, demands courage and instills insight, but one that leads to the zenith of self-fulfillment – where success is not an extrinsic reward but the inevitable consequence of aligning our actions with our authentic self. In the subsequent chapters, we shall explore further intricacies and strategies to positively leverage our identity to mold success habits and shape an invigorating life, steeped in purpose and illuminated by passion.

Thus, the meditative odyssey through the maze of identity is not merely the first stride, but a continuous journey. An ongoing expedition, further deepening our understanding of ourselves, maturing our identity constantly, allowing for its evolution with each passing experience. Keep this comprehension of identity close, for it is the solid core around which the other elements of success will persistently revolve.

Chapter 3. Chasing Passion: The Fuel of Purpose

Passion is a potent agent of transformation. It is an infectious energy that breathes life into the flanks of purpose and stirs the soul into a sense of invincibility. However, it isn't always presented on a silver platter. More often than not, it is a gleaming gem buried deep within the crust of fear, self-doubt, and the mundane. But when found, it fuels the purpose our lives yearn for.

3.1. The Concept of Passion-Fuelled Purpose

One might wonder what we mean by chasing passion. It isn't a race with a well-defined finish line we are talking about here. Chasing passion is more of a relentless quest for that spark that sets your soul ablaze and gives meaning to your every action. This spark, when united with the solid cornerstone of purpose, can make an ordinary life extraordinary!

Consider this, purpose is the firm ground upon which a structure stands, while passion is the fuel that lights up this majestic edifice, illuminating every brick, every corner, and every cavity. Purpose provides an undeniable "why" for the enduring journey of life, while passion fuels the "how," offering a vivacious boost that pushes us to defy odds and surmount obstacles.

Your passion might be for artistry, it might be for intellectual pursuits, for empowerment, for innovation, or even for compassion. Whatever your passions, remember that each of us is a unique tapestry woven with threads of myriad passions. No passion is too small or too insignificant as long as it fuels your purpose and supports you in the creation of your unique identity.

3.2. Unveiling Your Passion: The Journey Within

Chief among the tasks of chasing passion is the act of self-discovery. This journey within might be a daunting and convoluted path, but it is vital. Consider this journey as taking a deep dive into the oceanic depths of your soul. You might encounter dark abysses and scorching undercurrents during this dive. But herein lies the beauty. In these depths, amidst the highs and lows, your most authentic passions reside, silently pulsating and waiting to be discovered.

The inward journey begins by setting aside time for introspection. Reflect upon the activities, ideas, and people that stimulate a sense of joy and fulfillment within you. Contemplate on those moments that have left you in a state of 'flow,' where hours fly like minutes, and every second is infused with intense, heartfelt involvement. These are the telltale signs of passion, signs that signify a state of alignment between your core identity and your external reality.

Reconnect with these signs. Recharge your sense of self. This might involve revisiting old hobbies, exploring new interests, or even realigning your professional trajectory. Remember that neither age nor career constraints can influence this intrinsic chase of passion. It's all about the journey, the joy, and the jibes along the way. The goal is a life buoyed by passion, a life that side-steps mediocrity and offers a springboard into the waves of purposeful existence.

3.3. Harnessing Passion: The Next Steps

Once unveiled, the journey of passion doesn't end. It merely evolves into a more targeted pursuit, where passion must now be harnessed effectively to catalyze your purpose. Guiding this kind of passion-inspired pursuit requires intentionality, commitment, and the courage to wade through societal expectations and pressures.

Hence, it is crucial to set tangible goals linked to your passion. Goals that go beyond the boundaries of sheer ambition and instead tap into your passion reservoir. Prioritize the pursuit of these passion-quenching goals and weave them seamlessly into your everyday routines.

Allocate time to binge on your passion. Dedicate a part of your day to live, breathe, eat, and sleep your passion. This dedication might seem cumbersome at first, but soon, it will permeate your habits, your lifestyle, your identity, and, ultimately, your very existence.

Remember, harnessing passion is an ongoing dance with life, full of twists and twirls. But aim to be a dancer who sways smoothly to the tunes of passion, for a life steeped in passion is a life lived in purpose's brilliant hues!

3.4. Passion and Purpose: An Interdependent Duo

Finally, let us reiterate the symbiotic bond between passion and purpose. Passion without purpose risks dwindling into a state of restless fervor, while purpose without passion stares at the dreary prospect of a monotonous existence. Hence, the two are near inseparable companions on the journey to a well-defined identity.

Therefore, as we chase our passion and fuel our purpose, let us remind ourselves that while the path may be one of travail, the rewards far exceed the struggles. The ultimate reward, the grand finale, if you wish, of this ceaseless pursuit is anchored in the synchronicity of purpose and passion, a synchronicity that births an identity thriving in the richness of harnessed passions.

To sum up, the journey through the realms of passion begins with the discovery and unveiling of the passions that resonate with your deepest chords. It then evolves into a focused harnessing of these passions through purpose-driven goals and consistent practice. The finale of this passionate pursuit lies in the convergence of passion with purpose, resulting in a life brimming with vibrancy and enhanced by a solid sense of identity. Therefore, embrace the chase, courageously plunge into the depths of passion, and fuel the purpose that guides your path to success. The journey to your unique identity awaits!

Chapter 4. Moulding Habits with a Purpose: The Art and Science

The realization of our dreams and aspirations often hinges upon the daily habits we establish, which inform our actions and mindset. When these habits align with our purpose, they form a potent and powerful force that drives us towards not just success, but fulfillment. In this exploration of habit realignment, we delve into how we can consciously mould and utilize habits to pave the way for a life of profound meaning, purpose and exuberance.

4.1. How Habits Form and Function

The human mind is a fortress of complexity, nurturing an interwoven tapestry of thoughts, actions, and experiences that shape our identities. Key to understanding this maze is exploring how habits form and function.

Habits, in essence, act as mental shortcuts designed by our brains to save energy. They're often formed when the brain identifies a set pattern of stimuli followed by certain reactions. As a result of frequent repetition, our brains begin to automate responses to these stimuli, converting them into habits. From our morning ritual of brewing coffee to the evening regimen of brushing our teeth, habitual patterns weave through the fabric of our daily lives, often unbeknownst to us.

4.2. The Power of Purpose in Moulding Habits

Understanding habits necessitates exploration of purpose. Purpose is the force that fuels our passion, driving us to push boundaries, chase dreams, and ultimately achieve what may sometimes appear to be improbable. By infusing habits with purpose, our routine actions mutate into powerful catalysts for transformation.

When we consciously associate purpose with our habits, we begin to view them as not just monotonous tasks, but as significant steps towards our larger life goals. We transfigure the mundane into the magical, unveiling a world where each action is a step on the stepping stones to success.

4.3. The Art and Science of Habits

The process of moulding habits is where art meets science. Where science provides the structure and understanding of brain processes, art steps in with its creative prowess, allowing us to envision and construct habits that align with our higher self.

The science of habits necessitates awareness of our 'habit loop', a three-part process consisting of a cue, a routine, and a reward. Acknowledging specific actions tethered to habitual patterns enables us to effectively redirect behaviours, aligning them more with our purpose and desires.

The art, on the other hand, lies in creatively conceptualizing actions that could replace existing habits. This process transforms habits from mandatory routines to inspiring catalysts for change. Moreover, the introduction of unique rewards associated with new habits creates a sense of appeal, increasing the likelihood of sustained habit transformation.

4.4. Crafting Purposeful Habits: A Step-by-Step Guide

Infusing life with purposeful habits is an art form that beckons attention to detail, commitment, and patience. It's a journey, not a destination, and it's the small incremental changes that lead to monumental transformations over time. Let's break down this process into five critical steps:

1. Assess existing habits: Gain a comprehensive overview of your current habits. Observe patterns, triggers, and actions. What habits serve your purpose, and which ones veer you away?

2. Define your purpose: Clearly outline what drives you, what you aspire to achieve, and how you wish to impact the world.

3. Align habits with purpose: Identify which of your habits align with your central purpose and which you need to modify or replace.

4. Implement changes gradually: Start with small, manageable changes. As you gradually consolidate new habits, the change becomes seamless.

5. Reward and reinforce: Celebrate small victories. The reward system reinforces the habit loop, making the new action more appealing.

4.5. Conclusion: The Ongoing Journey of Habit Moulding

To mould habits with purpose, we must disentangle ourselves from the notion of rapid, overnight success. Habits are recurring patterns of behaviour that take time to alter, while purpose acts as the compass guiding this process. This journey demands persistence, resilience, and an open mind willing to learn, unlearn, and reshape habituated actions continuously.

By understanding the art and science of habit realignment, we can empower ourselves to progressively mould habits that are in sync with our purpose. In doing so, we step into a world where habits are a source of joy rather than a mere chore, driving us forward towards meaningful and purpose-fuelled progress. This is what lies at the heart of living authentically – embracing a relentless drive for success, and finding profound joy in the journey.

Chapter 5. Transforming Routines into Success Highways

In the enthralling quest of success, the routines we engross ourselves in play a significant role. They're like the main roads that lead us to our destination, the cherries of triumph that life has to offer. But remember, to direct these routine roads towards the highway of success, one must learn the art of transforming them optimally. It's nothing less than a blend of purpose, passion, discipline, determination, self-exploration, and conscious effort, meticulously woven together to craft an inspiring life tapestry. Hence, prepare to undertake a transcendent journey from routines to success highways.

5.1. The Foundation: Routines and Their Significance

Routines are repetitive actions or behavior patterns we find ourselves usually mired in, often leaving the most unconscious impressions on our lives. Some routines are essential (eating, sleeping), while others are optional (memes before bedtime). However, the magic lies not in the act but the consistency.

Have you ever noticed how brushing our teeth is second nature to us? It's an unmissable routine because we have practiced it incessantly since childhood. Such is the power of routines—what we do regularly and consistently; we become proficient at. Now imagine harnessing the same power, but this time, towards the objective of success! That's precisely what transforming routines into success highways entails.

5.2. The Tacit Agreement: Understanding the Interplay of Routines and Habits

To fully comprehend the transformation of routines into success highways, it's pivotal to recognize the subtle interplay between routines and habits. While routines are a structured series of actions, habits are behaviors performed almost automatically due to repeated enactment. They're like different sides of the same coin, feeding into each other in a cyclical manner. The secret sauce of success lies in molding our habits right, which indirectly shapes our routines, leading us closer to our goals.

5.3. The Conversion: Transforming Mundane Routines into Success-oriented Rituals

If routines are the foundation, transforming them into vehicles of success defines the building process. It starts with intention—changing routines for the better, creating a vision, and putting that spark of intention into action—a process called the Conversion.

To transform a routine into a success ritual, define its purpose, align it with your goal, and infuse it with passion. If your goal is fitness and your routine is waking up early, don't just wake up, transform it into an invigorating morning run. Now, the once 'mundane' act of waking up has concretely begun driving your highway of success.

5.4. The Lab Practice: Monitor, Modify, and Maintain

Transforming routines is a dynamic process, an experiment of sorts, requiring us to monitor our actions, modify the ones that don't work, and maintain the ones that do. It demands resilience, as initial setbacks are often unavoidable. But remember, each routine modified and maintained is a brick added to your success highway.

5.5. The Dynamic Duo: Consistency & Dedication

While routines are a set of regular activities, a success highway is the embodiment of growth, productivity, and achievement. The bridge linking these disparate concepts is the dynamic duo: consistency and dedication. Consistency ensures the regular practice of success-oriented routines, while dedication keeps us aligned with our goals even amidst adversities. The tandem of these traits helps us pave our success highways.

As we delve deeply into the process of transforming routines into success highways, it's crucial to remember that progress is always prized over perfection. The highway may not always be smooth or straight; there might be bends and bumps. But every inch moved forward, every routine transformed, is a step closer to success.

Embrace the beauty of this transformative journey and remember to celebrate the victories, no matter how small. After all, as Lao Tzu sagely said, "A journey of a thousand miles begins with a single step." You've already embarked on this phenomenal journey, and the path that lies ahead can only lead to fascinating discoveries and monumental triumphs.

Chapter 6. Harnessing Passion: Your Unique Motivational Source

Passion: It's a term frequently used but seldom fully harnessed. The journey to tapping its full potential begins by understanding what it genuinely means and identifying it within oneself. Passion refers to the zealous interest or intense desire one feels towards a particular subject or activity. Your passion isn't just a fleeting sensation — it's a profound force that monopolizes your thoughts, energizes your spirit, and draws you towards your goal, much like a magnetic pull. Undeniably, it is your unique motivational source.

6.1. Recognizing Your Passion

The initial step in the process of harnessing passion lies within the task of recognition. One must perceive their passion — the topic or activity that sets their heart alight, invigorates them, and inspires a sense of fulfilment. To identify your passion, educate yourself about every facet of your interests, projects, pursuits, and dreams that stir your emotions, fuel your curiosity, and motivate you to move mountains. You need to grasp the threads of your dreams and aspirations to see the broader image of passion that you've woven unknowingly. This exploration, while being a profound self-evaluation, offers an opportunity to uncover hidden realms of your personality, and it promotes a more intrinsic self-understanding, a prerequisite for harnessing passion effectively.

6.2. Channeling Passion towards Productive Outcomes

Perceiving passion within is not enough; one must channelize it towards productive outcomes. This process requires a strategy that places passion at the center of your thought-process, decision-making, and daily routines. Several ways exist to accomplish this, including the frequent engagement in activities related to the passion domain, setting specific goals aligned with it, and ensuring these goals trickle down to daily responsibilities and tasks. Regular mindfulness exercises also aid in keeping the passion flame burning sincerely and consistently.

The robust implementation of these steps guarantees the transformation of raw, unchecked passion into a powerhouse of persistent motivation driving you towards your goals. One must, however, remember that this process is gradual and requires consistent effort, perseverance, and meticulous nurturing of your passion.

6.3. Passion as a Motivational Source

In grappling with the complexities of life, one's resolve may falter. This is where the power of passion comes into play. As an individual-specific motivational source, it serves to rejuvenate one's spirit, rekindle one's interest, and refurbish one's zest. Remarkably, the passion-infused drive to achieve isn't merely about reaching the destination but also about the thrill of the journey itself. This perspective fosters an organic growth mindset, encouraging continuous learning, resilience in the face of setbacks, and the repeated refining of skills - all critical components of lifelong success.

Yet, it's vital to note that while passion forms a dynamic motivational source, its intensity can vary. Periods of low motivation are not indicative of lost passion; they are mere 'ebb and flow'. During these 'ebb' phases, the key is to dispel self-doubt, anchor oneself in their belief system, and keep moving.

6.4. The Balance: Passion and Logical Decision-Making

While passion serves as a powerful motivator, there is a pitfall to steer clear from – the overwhelming surge of passion that clouds one's logical thought process. While it's vital to let passion lead, maintaining a healthy balance between passion-driven actions and logical decision-making is just as crucial. This delicate balance pushes you to pursue your passion, yet also keeps you grounded with the practicalities and realities of life.

Be excited by your passion but remember to keep an eye on the finer elements of planning and execution, continuously revising and adjusting your course as necessary. A balanced approach allows you to pursue your passion while staying firmly rooted in reality — a crucial aspect often overlooked in the pursuit of success. Proactively seeking feedback, implementing it, and envisioning different perspectives will aid in maintaining this equilibrium.

Harnessing your passion is, in essence, about leveraging it as your unique motivational source. It compels one to strive for greatness, keeping them firmly focused on their path, filled with demanding challenges and exhilarating victories. As you continue to fuel your passion, it becomes a ceaseless source of energy, inspiring you to move forward and enabling you to craft your success habits with purpose and fervor. As you delve deeper into your passion and align it with your identity and purpose, you indeed shape a triumphant triad, paving the way towards an exceptionally prosperous, passion-fuelled life.

Chapter 7. Interconnecting Identity, Purpose and Passion: The Triad of Triumph

To understand the profound connection and harmonious interplay that exists between our identity, purpose, and passion, we must first dissect each component of this triumvirate and examine how they intertwine to form a sturdy, triumphant triad.

7.1. Sculpting the Sculptor: Understanding Identity

Our identity is the sum total of our thoughts, emotions, values, skills and beliefs; it is the conscious awareness of our unique existence. It can be argued that identity is the basis of our individuality - the bedrock upon which our character is crafted. When we scrutinize ourselves, the resulting identity can be greatly diverse from who we perceived ourselves to be initially. Understanding and establishing this identity is paramount before we can interact meaningfully with our purpose and passion.

Identity, in essence, is the self-realized, self-identified representation of our natural skill set, our emotional responses, and our instinctive unconscious considerations. To continuously thrive and evolve, it is of utmost importance to reflect upon, scrutinize, and mold our identity. This self-awareness allows us to channel our energy towards our purpose and passion more deliberately, leading to an exponential magnification of opportunities to achieve success.

7.2. Destination Defined: The True Essence of Purpose

The next cog in our triad is purpose. Think of your life as a journey. Your purpose would be the destination of this journey, the endgame, the objective your heart yearns to accomplish. It is the driving force that propels our existence and furnishes meaning to our lives. Upon understanding and accepting our identity, we develop the capacity to comprehend our purpose - to understand the why behind our actions, choices, and decisions.

A clearly defined purpose can make the difference between mere existence and truly living. Equipped with a profound understanding of our purpose, we become resolved and focused, effectively channeling our resources, efforts, and time toward the realization of our ambitions. With a clear purpose in mind, even daunting obstacles transform into stepping stones that direct us towards our vision of success.

7.3. Ignite the Flame: Recognizing Passion

Passion, the third pivotal element of our triumphant triad, is that potent, invincible power that fuels our actions and sustains our motivation. It is the irresistibly magnetic force that draws us towards certain activities, subjects or causes, filling us with an insatiable eagerness and a fervent zeal. It's the unquenchable fire that not only enkindles but also sustains our journey towards our purpose.

Passion works hand in hand with purpose, providing the essential energy to pursue our goals relentlessly. When harnessed appropriately, passion can stimulate creativity, enforce dedication, and instill resilience - key ingredients in the recipe for success.

7.4. The Triad of Triumph: A Confluence of Identity, Purpose, and Passion

We can now dissect how our identity, purpose, and passion harmonize within the triumphant triad. Our identity forms the foundation, directing us towards understanding our capabilities, strengths, and areas of expertise. Recognizing our identity furnishes the critical comprehension needed for forming a resonant and meaningful purpose - the grand objective that motivates our actions and pursuits. Lastly, once our purpose has been birthed from our identity's realization, passion can fuel the journey towards accomplishing that purpose, supplementing the necessary zeal, perseverance and tenacity.

This triumvirate acts as a compass guiding us through our life's voyage, steering us onto the path that aligns most authentically with our individuality and energizes us towards our goal. Harnessing the power of this triad forms the basis of successful existence, leading to self-fulfillment, personal development, and some would argue, an enlightened state of self-actualization.

By assiduously cultivating an understanding of our identity, defining our purpose, and kindling our passion, we equip ourselves with a potent tool-set to craft success habits, establish significant milestones, and follow through on our most ambitious goals. Intricately interwoven, our identity, purpose, and passion create the triumphant triad, empowering us to shape not just our habits, but our whole lifestyle, in alignment with our true self and aspirations. A life lived in resonance with this triad is truly a life well-lived. It not only enhances our personal existence but also influences those around us positively, creating a ripple effect which triggers growth and development globally.

Chapter 8. Building Resilience: The Power of Focused Identity

Resilience, a trait often associated with endurance and the ability to bounce back in times of adversity, plays a pivotal role in the journey of self-development and success. Analysing resilience from the perspective of a focused identity involves understanding how a clear sense of self can amplify one's resilience, and subsequently, the effectiveness of one's habits.

8.1. The Link Between Resilience and Identity

Endurance, determination, fortitude – these are often the elements that come to the forefront when we talk about resilience. But, from a broader perspective, resilience is reinforced by notions of identity. With a clear, focused identity, a person can withstand trials and tribulations with grit and grace. This union between a focussed identity and resilience is seamless, yet dynamic. When an individual has a clear understanding of their identity, it allows them to lean towards consistency, thus fuelling their resilience. Consistency, here, acts as the glue binding together the elements of one's identity, resulting in an unwavering force against life's unpredictable nuances.

8.2. The Power of Focused Identity

Identity, when subjected to focus, becomes a power in itself. A specific understanding of oneself aids individuals in defining their pursuits, thereby fashioning their habits around these pursuits. An individual with a focused identity displays a greater understanding of their abilities and limitations. This understanding manifests as strength in overcoming adversity and hurdling obstacles that might arise in their path. A well-defined self-identity leads to self-reliance, which is another facet of resilience. Being able to rely on one's self is an indication of a strong, resilient personality.

8.3. Fostering Resilience Through Purpose and Habits

A focused identity is often paired with a purpose-driven mindset. When purpose is coupled with resilience, it becomes a beacon, guiding individuals through their life's journey. This guiding force provides a sense of direction in building and sustaining productive habits. As individuals tailor their habits around their purpose, these habits act as supportive pillars adding structure to their resilient nature. It's much simpler to be resilient when actions and habits are purposeful, as the objective is clearly visible and transparent, serving as a motivational force in times of difficulty.

8.4. Overcoming Life's Obstacles with Resilience

In the face of adversity, a focused identity fortified with resilience stands as a powerful determinant of one's ability to bounce back. Life presents numerous challenges, but approaching them with a robust sense of self can be advantageous. By grounding oneself in their identity and steering their life trajectory toward their defined goals, one can traverse these challenging situations with effortless resilience. This resilience, colored by focused identity, serves as a tool to maneuver through life's ambiguity, making way for growth and personal development.

8.5. The Role of Passion in Strengthening Resilience

Passion can be considered a catalyst in refining resilience. An individual bubbling with passion for their dreams is naturally inclined towards developing a robust identity that potentiates resilience. With passion, their identity takes on a radiant glow, their purpose becomes more focused, and their resilience amplified. Here, passion is the driving force that propels individuals forward, enabling them to withstand hardships and bounce back from failures.

8.6. Synthesizing Resilience for a Promising Future

Resilience, when maximized through a focused identity, becomes a beacon of personal growth and success. Individuals with a resilient mindset and a clear identity tend to effectively channel their passions into fruitful habits, lending them a leg up in their pursuit of success. In embracing resilience, one unlocks vast opportunities for growth and enriches their life with purpose and passion.

In conclusion, the journey of crafting success habits with purpose and passion is working in tandem with resilience and identity. Possessing a focused identity promotes resilience, strengthening an individual's ability to surmount hardships and emerge triumphant. Moulding resilient personalities with focused identities, this chapter sparks a new understanding, enlightening the journey of passion, purpose, and persistence.

Chapter 9. From Habits to Lifestyle: Crafting a Relentless Pursuit of Success

The journey from habits to a lifestyle is, by all accounts, a voyage of transformation. This chapter placidly unravels the intricate processes involved in this pivotal transition and gears you up towards constructing a relentless pursuit of success. It carves a path that aids in reshaping your everyday habits into a robust lifestyle of success, ensured to catalyze far-reaching repercussions - the ones that echo back as trophies of triumph.

9.1. From The Ground Up: Building Habits Block By Block

When we speak about habits, we're fundamentally talking about a series of actions that you routinely carry out, often unconsciously. Habits could be small, like brushing your teeth first thing in the morning, or significant, like dedicating an hour to reading or self-development daily. The power of habits lies in their capacity to elicit monumental results when persistently followed.

Shaping habits first demands acknowledging the fundamental components of a habit. Behavior analysts often describe a habit as a three-part process: the cue or trigger that precipitates the action, the routine or action itself, and finally, the reward derived thereof. Being aware of these components can provide leverage to control and mold your habits. Adopt the habits that serve your higher purpose and replace those which deviate you from your path.

9.2. The Ladder of Progress: Scaling From Habits to Lifestyle

Habits in isolation might appear negligible. Yet, when you place those same habits in a broader perspective, they begin to illuminate their true power. They build upon each other, weaving an intricate tapestry that reflects the larger manifestation of your lifestyle. Climbing this ladder from habits to a lifestyle, you must strategically convert your purpose-driven habits into patterns ingrained into your being.

Start by aligning your habits with your identity, purpose, and passion. Then, incorporate them into your everyday regimen until they become your second nature. Ensure this transition by reinforcing the rewards and incentives related to each habit. It is necessary to keep positively reinforcing your habits to affirm that they are not just ticking items off a to-do list, but forming the cornerstone of your ultimate lifestyle.

9.3. Craft An Unrelenting Pursuit of Success

Cultivating a lifestyle requires firm resolve, persistent effort, and, most importantly, consistency. It's equivalent to sculpting a statue. Each habit you adopt is like a chisel on a block of marble, shaping and refining it until it finally reveals the masterpiece within.

Embarking on this journey, remember three key elements that stimulate a relentless pursuit of success. Firstly, perseverance - the ability to maintain focus and direction regardless of challenges. Secondly, elasticity - the capacity to retract from setbacks and bounce back even stronger. Lastly, consistency - the uniformity in maintaining your positive habits even amidst adversities.

9.4. Upholding Your Success-Focused Lifestyle With Stewardship

Once you've established a lifestyle aligned to success, the next crucial step is stewardship. Stewardship implies an attitude of responsibility, the willingness to continually improve, refine, and maintain the lifestyle you've created. It requires you to perpetually examine and tweak your habits, ensuring they're serving your ultimate goals of success efficiently.

Regular self-reflection exercises can prove instrumental in this process. Practice asking yourself how a habit is contributing towards your purpose and identify areas of improvement. Use this enhanced awareness to refine your habits, and by extension, your lifestyle, enhancing its relevance and effectiveness in your relentless pursuit of success.

In essence, to transform habits into a success-oriented lifestyle, integrate your purpose-driven habits into an intricate fabric of daily actions. Nurture this transformation by consistently practicing your habits, maintaining a positive attitude, displaying resilience, and exercising stewardship of your adopted lifestyle. The gateway to an energized, passion-fueled, purposeful life lies open: the choice and the journey to walk through it, is unequivocally yours.

Chapter 10. Nurturing a Passion-Driven Life: Secrets Unveiled

Commencing our exploration into nurturing a passion-driven life, we set out on a journey brimming with the promise of discovery and self-realization. Truly, the pursuit of a passion-driven life is like a voyage on an immense ocean, filled with both calm seas and roiling storms. Regardless of the weather, seasoned sailors maintain their course, using their passion as a steady compass to navigate the challenges that may arise.

10.1. Harnessing and Channeling Your Passion

The first and perhaps most critical step in fostering a life driven by ardor is the task of genuinely comprehending your passion and learning how to funnel it effectively. Picture your passion as a raw, energetic force, thriving within the core of your being. This unembellished power must be carefully honed and channeled adequately to achieve desirable outcomes.

In order to harness this intrinsic energy, it is crucial to introspect and sketch out a clear understanding of your passion. What truly sparks joy within you? What ignites that uncontainable fire in your heart and leaves you with an insatiable appetite for more? When you know and understand these visceral experiences, you then possess the key to unlocking your life's purpose.

However, understanding your passion alone does not complete the task. The next phase is to channel it. Envision a flooding river, its waters powerful and swift. Without proper channels to guide it, this mighty flow could wreak havoc. But when properly guided through well-designed channels, it can irrigate vast lands, generate electrical power, and support an array of life. Similarly, your passion, when channeled through the right pursuits that align with your identity and purpose, can be transformational, impacting your life and the lives around you positively.

10.2. Converting Passion into Productivity

When passion is appropriately leveraged, it becomes a formidable tool for productivity. Take to heart, a millionaire is not passionate about amassing wealth because of the numbers in his bank account. Instead, the stock trader or the real estate mogul are passionate about the process of making deals, strategizing, mitigating risks, and ultimately creating value.

To truly convert passion into productivity, the focus should be committed to the process rather than the outcome. A disciplined approach towards executing individual tasks, appreciating small wins, and dedicating oneself to continuous learning and improvement can have an immense impact on productivity levels. Meanwhile, failures and setbacks should be dealt with resilience, and viewed as stepping stones or moments for learning and growth.

10.3. The Role of Goals in a Passion-Driven Life

In a passion-driven life, having clear and well-set goals can act like lighthouses, casting a light upon your path and guiding you towards your purpose even amidst the darkest storms. The integration of your goals and passion provides a sturdy framework within which your true potential can flourish.

However, while setting goals, it's important to ensure that they are SMART - Specific, Measurable, Attainable, Relevant, and Time-bound. Goals refined by such parameters ensure clarity of thought, focused efforts, and efficient time management, thereby catapulting you towards your desired success.

10.4. Maintaining Balance: Passion and Practicality

It is imperative to remember that living a passion-driven life does not warrant shunning practicality. A robust set of practical skills is essential in turning dreams into reality. Understanding finances, crafting strategies, improving communication, and organization skills all play significant roles in translating passion into palpable success. Embrace a micro approach towards passion, refining it with practical skill sets and gradually building a stable bridge between your dreams and reality.

10.5. Cultivating a Growth Mindset

Ultimately, nurturing a passion-driven life requires the cultivation of a growth mindset. Absorb challenges, setbacks, and criticisms as mere pitstops on your journey towards success. Constant learning, adapting to new situations, and venturing out of your comfort zone are all attributes of a growth mindset. It is in this fertile soil of unending personal development that the seeds of a passion-driven life can truly blossom.

In conclusion, the journey of nurturing a passion-driven life is filled with discovery, introspection, dedicated efforts, and constant learning. It involves balancing passion with practicality, channeling energy into productivity, and cultivating a growth mindset. However, More than anything, it is a lifelong commitment to your own self, a vow to lead a life driven by the soulful essence of the things you love, the things that set your spirit roaring with an uncontainable power. Truly, to walk this path is to taste the magic of a fulfilling, radiant, and successful life.

Chapter 11. Reflections and Upkeep: Keeping Your Identity, Purpose and Passion Aligned

Sustaining an unbroken alignment between one's identity, purpose, and passion may seem challenging, yet the rewards reaped from this concerted interplay can be truly monumental. This chapter is a deep exploration of the disciplined practice of continued contemplation and consistent maintenance, crucial to safeguarding the harmonized relationship among your purpose, passion, and personal identity.

11.1. The Vicious or Virtuous: The Cycle of Reflective Practice

Begin by visualizing personal reflection as a circle, where the entry point is any moment of introspection about who you are, what your passions are, and your life's purpose. Reflection could involve meditations on recent actions, how those merged or diverged from your defined identity, or how well they served your purpose or expressed your passion.

Reflection is more than a mere afterthought. It's an active process requiring consistent effort, where one cogitates on their experiences, evaluates their responses, digests the lessons, and plans for future situations. Yet, this justifies virtually half the circle of reflective practice. The experience of self-reflection transforms into an incessant virtuous circle only when it leads to self-improvement.

Through this lens of enhanced self-awareness, we can appraise our actions, decisions, and underlying thought processes. Recognize any incongruities between intentions and behaviors; engross yourself in rectifying interceptions distortive of your identity, purpose, or passion. Such deliberate efforts glue the key aspects of your existence together into a coherent and powerful whole.

11.2. Consistent Upkeep: Fortifying the Alignment

Sustaining alignment isn't accomplished merely by setting goals, finding your passion and identifying your purpose. Consistent upkeep involves regular check-ins with oneself, ensuring an ever-present and vigilant upkeeping of alignment in an ever-evolving context. This upkeep could be as simple as daily journaling or as involved as a full-day personal retreat or a session with a life coach every few months.

Remember that you're an evolving being living in a dynamic world. With time, your identity may morph, your passion can change lanes, the purpose that gives your life meaning today might be replaced by another in due course. Algernon Charles Swinburne rightly said, "Man changes life and Fortune changes man". Therefore, the consistency isn't just about keeping your identity, purpose, and passion aligned, but also about regularly revisiting these aspects of self, acknowledging changes and realigning them continually.

11.3. Adjust, Adapt, Advance: The Triple A's of Upkeep

The alignment between identity, passion, and purpose isn't about sticking to a pre-defined path with unwavering rigidity - it's about flexibility. 'Adjust, Adapt, Advance,' the triple-A mantra, instills this elasticity into our upkeep routine.

The ability to adjust involves the willingness to tweak our way of doing things, be it a style of work, habit patterns or our perspectives. Adapting involves improvement and transformation based on the lessons learned from our experiences, while advancing is about forward motion, perpetual growth and development.

The application of this triple-A mantra ensures that our personal identity, passion, and purpose aren't just rigid entities; they are, conversely, evolving dimensions that are as fluid as we allow them to be. The dynamic nature of the triple-A's allows us to keep abreast of these changes in a healthy and balanced manner.

11.4. Reflections and Upkeep: A Symphony of Continuity

Concluding, the maintenance of alignment between one's identity, purpose, and passion is not a one-time event, but a lifelong process and a rhythmic dance of continuity. Through 'Reflections and Upkeep,' you become the skilled choreographer of your life's ballet. You orchestrate an entrancing dance that is in striking harmony with your true self, your fiery passions, and your purpose that brings meaning to your existence.

Remember that you are a masterpiece and a work in progress simultaneously. This chapter illustrates how the regular practice of reflection and the ceaseless upkeep of alignment are fundamental in maintaining the integrity of this beautiful interplay, enabling you to lead an intoxicating life filled with purpose, passion, and a pristine sense of identity.